STORNOWAY PRIMARY

WESTERN ISLES LIBRARIES

Readers are requested to take great care of the books while in their possession, and to point out any defects that they may notice in them to the Librarian.

This book is issued for a period of twenty-one days and should be returned on or before the latest date stamped below, but an extension of the period of loan may be granted when desired.

DATE OF RETURN	DATE OF RETURN	DATE OF RETURN
. . . .	. . . .	. . . .
. . . .	. . . .	. . . .
. . . .	. . . .	. . . .
. . . .	. . . .	. . . .
. . . .	. . . .	. . . .
. . . .	. . . .	. . . .
. . . .	. . . .	. . . .
. . . .	. . . .	. . . .
. . . .	. . . .	. . . .
. . . .	. . . .	. . . .
. . . .	. . . .	. . . .
. . . .	. . . .	. . . .
. . . .	. . . .	. . . .

ASK ISAAC ASIMOV ?

How do big ships float?

Heinemann

First published in Great Britain by Heinemann Library
an imprint of Heinemann Publishers (Oxford) Ltd
Halley Court, Jordan Hill, Oxford OX2 8EJ

OXFORD LONDON EDINBURGH MADRID
ATHENS BOLOGNA PARIS MELBOURNE
SYDNEY AUCKLAND SINGAPORE TOKYO
IBADAN NAIROBI HARARE GABORONE
PORTSMOUTH NH (USA)

98 97 96 95 94

10 9 8 7 6 5 4 3 2 1

British Library Cataloguing in Publication Data is available from the British Library on request.

ISBN 0 431 07646 4

Cover designed and pages typeset by Philip Parkhouse
Printed in China

Picture Credits
pp. 2-3, © Kirk Schlea/Picture Perfect USA; pp. 4-5, © J. E. Stevenson/Robert Harding Picture Library; pp. 6-7 © Bernard Régent/Hutchinson Library; pp. 8-9, © Dick Wade/Picture Perfect USA; pp.10-11, © Kirk Schlea/Picture Perfect USA; pp. 12-13, Tom Redman, 1992; pp. 14-15, © Ken Novak, 1992; pp. 16-17, © Fritz Prenzel/Bruce Coleman Limited; p. 17 (inset) © Mary Evans Picture Library; pp. 18-19, Courtesy of CSX Corporation; pp. 20-21, © Kirk Schlea/Picture Perfect USA; pp. 22-23, © Dr. Eckart Pott/ Bruce Coleman Limited; p. 24, © Dr. Eckart Pott/Bruce Coleman Limited

Cover photograph © Greg Evans Photo Library
Back cover photograph © Sygma/D. Kirkland

The book designer wishes to thank Jim and Ginger Montella from Blue Ribbon Pets, Inc., Milwaukee, Wisconsin, and the models for their cooperation.

Series editor: Valerie Weber
Editors: Barbara J. Behm and Patricia Lantier-Sampon
Series designer: Sabine Beaupré
Book designer: Kristi Ludwig
Picture researcher: Diane Laska

Contents

Words that appear in the glossary are printed in **bold** the first time they occur in the text.

Modern-day wonders

Pick up your telephone and you can have a conversation with someone halfway round the world. Turn on your video-recorder and you can watch a television programme that was shown last night after you had gone to bed. These are only some of the many wonders of **technology**.

Big ships are another amazing scientific achievement. Some ships today are as large as a small town. How do big ships float? Let's find out.

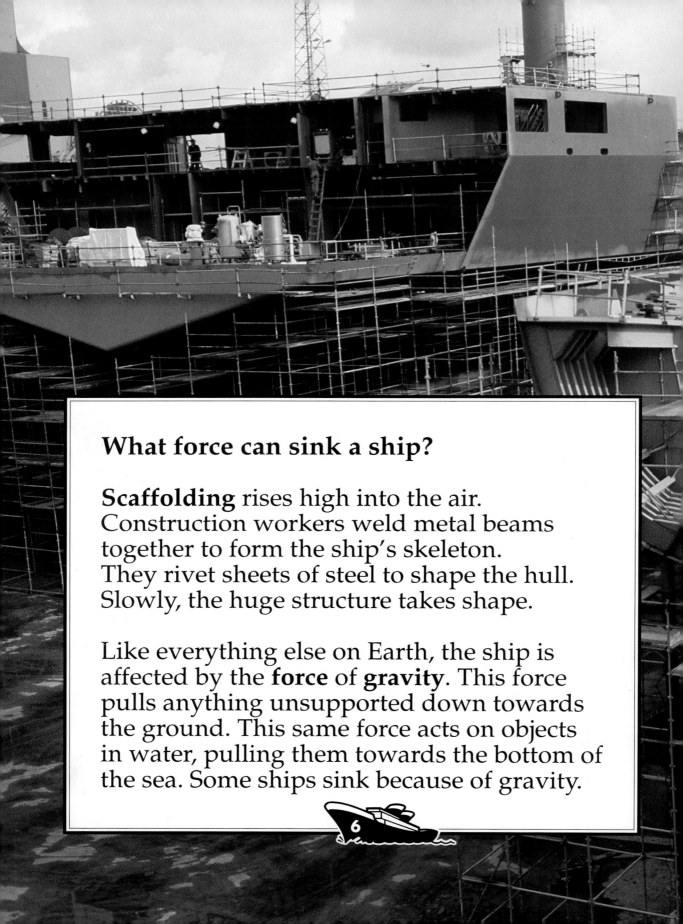

What force can sink a ship?

Scaffolding rises high into the air.
Construction workers weld metal beams
together to form the ship's skeleton.
They rivet sheets of steel to shape the hull.
Slowly, the huge structure takes shape.

Like everything else on Earth, the ship is
affected by the **force** of **gravity**. This force
pulls anything unsupported down towards
the ground. This same force acts on objects
in water, pulling them towards the bottom of
the sea. Some ships sink because of gravity.

6

Why do some things float?

It is a beautiful day, and you decide to go swimming. Sitting in an inner tube, you relax in the water. The river's gentle current pulls you along. With the aid of the inner tube, you float effortlessly on the water. Water pushes up on anything placed in it. The upward push of the water is called the **buoyant force**. When the buoyant force is strong enough to overcome the force of gravity on an object, the object floats.

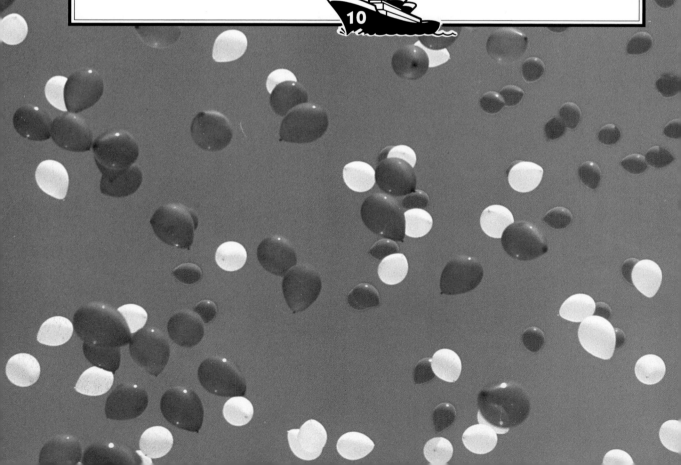

Sink or float?

You watch, sadly, as your colourful balloon rises towards the clouds. You have let go of the string, and the balloon has escaped into the air. A balloon floats upwards if it is full of helium, a gas which is lighter than air. Objects float in water for a similar reason: they are lighter than water.

But it is not as simple as it sounds. A rolled-up sheet of steel sinks. But when the same steel is shaped into the **hull** of a ship, it floats.

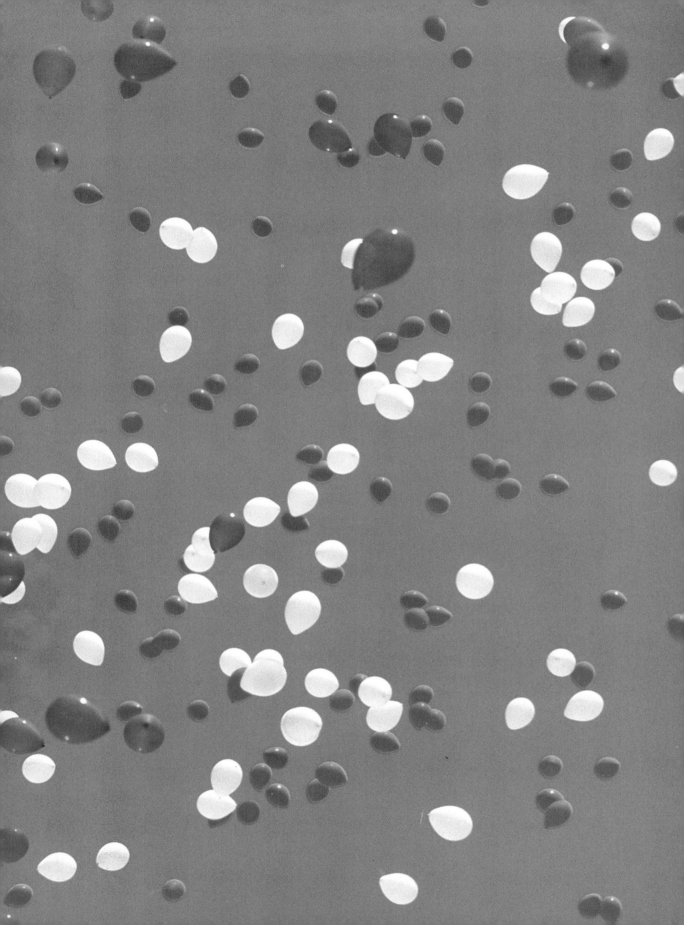

Why is a ship's density important?

An object's **volume** – the amount of space it takes up – combined with its **weight** determines whether it will sink or float. The ship's hull, including the air it encloses, takes up more space than the roll of steel. This means that the weight of the steel is spread over a larger volume. In other words, the ship's **density** is less than the density of the roll of steel. In fact, the ship is less dense than water. Anything less dense than water floats. Anything more dense sinks.

Prove it yourself

Shape some clay into a ball and place it in water. Does it float? Now, shape the clay into a hollow boat. Place your boat in the water. The weight of the clay is spread out over a larger area of water. Its density is less than that of water, so your boat will float. But if your boat has a hole in it, it will take on water. This will add too much weight, and the boat will sink.

14

What happened to the *Titanic*?

One of the world's most famous ships is at the bottom of the sea. The *Titanic* sank on its first voyage in 1912 after hitting an iceberg. This huge luxury liner has been found on the floor of the Atlantic Ocean. Many of its ornate decorations still remain.

The *Queen Elizabeth 2* is a luxury liner whose fate has been far luckier. Her passengers can enjoy the luxuries of a swimming pool, theatre, nightclubs and a shopping arcade on cruises across the Atlantic Ocean.

White Star triple-screw steamer "Titanic", 45,000 tons, which sank on April 15th 1912 with 1,635 people.

How big is a supertanker?

The *Queen Elizabeth 2* is small compared to a supertanker. The luxury liner is 294 metres long and can hold 60,000 tonnes. A supertanker can carry almost ten times that much. Its only cargo is oil.

Supertankers are the world's largest ships. They are so large they can dock at only a few ports. Usually, supertankers are unloaded far from shore by using underwater pipes or by transferring their oil to smaller ships.

Which ships can sink and float?

Some ships are useful not because they float, but because they sink. **Submarines** take in water through special chambers, allowing them to sink. They can dive down to the ocean floor and cruise along.

To rise back to the surface, the submarine forces out the water it contains. **Compressed** air is pumped into the chambers, making the submarine less dense than the water. The ship becomes buoyant and rises to the surface.

20

From ripples to waves

From delicate ripples on a starlit pond to thundering waves on stormy seas, water fascinates us in all its forms. Thanks to our understanding of what makes things float, we have been able to build ships of all kinds. We can now safely enjoy and explore the world's lakes, oceans and waterways.

22

Glossary

buoyant force: the force that results from water pushing up on an object. If the buoyant force is strong enough to counteract gravity, the object floats.

compressed: forced to occupy a smaller space than normal

density: the weight of an object divided by its volume

force: a push or pull that changes an object's speed or the direction in which it is moving

gravity: the force that pulls everything towards the centre of the Earth

hull: the body of a ship, not including the masts, sails, rigging, deck or buildings on the deck

scaffolding: a temporary platform for workers to stand or sit on when working above the floor or ground

submarine: a ship that can cruise underwater

technology: the use of scientific principles to produce things which are useful to people

volume: the amount of space an object takes up

weight: the measure of how heavy an object is

23

Index

24